I Feel Happy

Kelly Doudna

Published by SandCastle™, an imprint of ABDO Publishing Company, 4940 Viking Drive, Edina, Minnesota 55435.

Printed in the United States.

Photo credits: Adobe Image Library, Corel, Digital Stock, Digital Vision, MasterClips, PhotoDisc

Library of Congress Cataloging-in-Publication Data

Doudna, Kelly, 1963-
    I feel happy / Kelly Doudna.
       p. cm. -- (How do you feel?)
    Summary: In photographs and simple text, children tell what makes
them feel happy, such as a puppy and spending time with Grandpa.
    ISBN 1-57765-188-X
    1. Happiness in children--Juvenile literature. [1. Happiness.]
I. Title. II. Series: Doudna, Kelly, 1963- How do you feel?
BF723.H37D68 1998
152.4'2--dc21
                                    98-26675
                                         CIP
                                         AC

The SandCastle concept, content, and reading method have been reviewed and approved by a national advisory board including literacy specialists, librarians, elementary school teachers, early childhood education professionals, and parents.

Let Us Know

After reading the book, SandCastle would like you to tell us your stories about reading. What is your favorite page? Was there something hard that you needed help with? Share the ups and downs of learning to read. We want to hear from you! To get posted on the Abdo Publishing Company Web site, send us email at:

sandcastle@abdopub.com

About SandCastle™

Nonfiction books for the beginning reader

- Basic concepts of phonics are incorporated with integrated language methods of reading instruction. Most words are short, and phrases, letter sounds, and word sounds are repeated.

- Readability is determined by the number of words in each sentence, the number of characters in each word, and word lists based on curriculum frameworks.

- Full-color photography reinforces word meanings and concepts.

- "Words I Can Read" list at the end of each book teaches basic elements of grammar, helps the reader recognize the words in the text, and builds vocabulary.

- Reading levels are indicated by the number of flags on the castle.

Look for more SandCastle books
in these three reading levels:

Level 1 (one flag)	Level 2 (two flags)	Level 3 (three flags)
Grades Pre-K to K	Grades K to 1	Grades 1 to 2
5 or fewer words per page	5 to 10 words per page	10 to 15 words per page

I feel happy when the day is sunny and the birds sing.

I feel happy when I play with balloons.

What makes you happy?

I feel happy when I play
with a clown at a party.

I feel happy when I play with a friendly dog.

When I feel happy, I sing so loud that my friend covers her ears.

I feel happy when my friend and I swim on a hot day.

I feel happy when Grandpa helps me ride my new bike.

I feel happy when Dad and
I have a tea party.

I feel happy because I have friends who are fun.

Words I Can Read

Nouns

A noun is a person, place, or thing

bike (BIKE) p. 17
clown (KLOWN) p. 9
Dad (DAD) p. 19
day (DAY) pp. 5, 15
dog (DAWG) p. 11
friend (FREND) pp. 13, 15

Grandpa
  (GRAND-pah) p. 17
party (PAR-tee) p. 9
tea party
  (TEE par-tee) p. 19

Plural Nouns

A plural noun is more than one
person, place, or thing

balloons
  (buh-LOONZ) p. 7
birds (BURDZ) p. 5

ears (IHRZ) p. 13
friends (FRENDZ) p. 21

Pronouns

A pronoun is a word that replaces a noun

I (EYE) pp. 5, 7, 9, 11, 13, 15,
  17, 19, 21
me (MEE) p. 17

who (HOO) p. 21
you (YOO) p. 7

22

Verbs

A verb is an action or being word

are (AR) p. 21
covers (KUHV-urz) p. 13
feel (FEEL) pp. 5, 7, 9, 11, 13, 15, 17, 19, 21
have (HAV) pp. 19, 21
helps (HELPSS) p. 17

is (IZ) p. 5
makes (MAYKSS) p. 7
play (PLAY) pp. 7, 9, 11
ride (RIDE) p. 17
sing (SING) pp. 5, 13
swim (SWIM) p. 15

Adjectives

An adjective describes something

friendly (FREND-lee) p. 11
fun (FUHN) p. 21
happy (HAP-ee) pp. 5, 7, 9, 11, 13, 15, 17, 19, 21
her (HUR) p. 13

hot (HOT) p. 15
my (MYE) pp. 13, 15, 17
new (NOO) p. 17
sunny (SUHN-ee) p. 5

Adverbs

An adverb tells how, when, or where something happens

loud (LOWD) p. 13

so (SOH) p. 13

23

Glossary

balloons - Small bags made of thin
rubber that are filled with air or gas.

clown - A person who wears funny
clothes, has a painted face, and
makes people laugh.

friend - Someone you like being with
and know well.

tea party - A group of people who
have tea together.